CLONE TROOPERS

WRITTEN BY HANNAH DOLAN, ELIZABETH DOWSETT, CLARE HIBBERT, SHARI LAST, AND VICTORIA TAYLOR

INTRODUCTION

The brave clone troopers are ready to defend the LEGO® *Star Wars* galaxy. While they may all be clones of Jango Fett, they have different personalities and specialized equipment.

HOW TO USE THIS BOOK

These amazing minifigures are ordered according to the *Star Wars*™ property in which they first appeared or mostly featured. Tabs at the top of each page indicate which properties this minifgure appears in. As most *Star Wars* characters appear in the wider universe of Legends, that tab is highlighted only if a minifigure appears in an Legends set. The Clone Wars tab has not been highlighted if the character has a separate Clone Wars minifigure.

This book also includes variants of featured minifigures, which are the same character, but have some modifications that make them different in some way.

Contents

The Phase I clone trooper is part of a vast army that has been cloned from a single individual. Sealed in a shell of white armor, his minifigure first appears in Episode II sets in 2002. During the Clone Wars, his armor becomes lighter and more adaptable, with diverse color markings to denote different ranks. The most recent update is sleeker still.

STAR VARIANT
Clone Trooper Episode II
This Phase I Clone Trooper from 2002's Republic Gunship (set 7163) is the first of his kind. Under his helmet is a faceless black head.

Clone Trooper
GENETICALLY MODIFIED SOLDIER

Blast from the past
The Phase I clone trooper's blaster is a LEGO® loudhailer with a translucent blue round plate attached. LEGO *Star Wars* minifigures carried this blaster until bespoke LEGO *Star Wars* blasters were released in 2007.

The 2013 clone trooper has a new helmet, and under it a new identity— the grimacing face of a clone

Subtle details on standard trooper armor

Utility belt carries clone trooper survival gear

DATA FILE
YEAR: 2013
FIRST SET: 75000 Clone Troopers vs. Droidekas
NO. OF SETS: 5
PIECES: 4
ACCESSORIES: Blaster

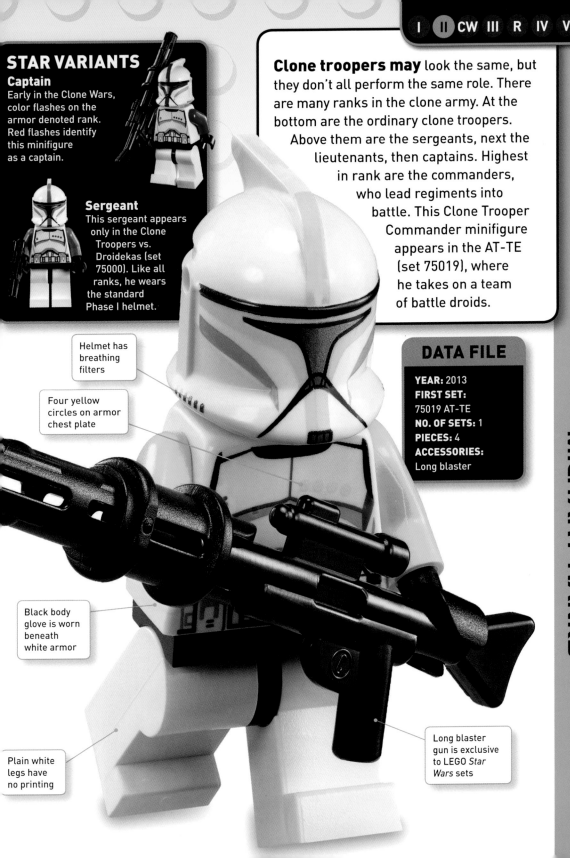

STAR VARIANTS

Captain
Early in the Clone Wars, color flashes on the armor denoted rank. Red flashes identify this minifigure as a captain.

Sergeant
This sergeant appears only in the Clone Troopers vs. Droidekas (set 75000). Like all ranks, he wears the standard Phase I helmet.

Clone troopers may look the same, but they don't all perform the same role. There are many ranks in the clone army. At the bottom are the ordinary clone troopers. Above them are the sergeants, next the lieutenants, then captains. Highest in rank are the commanders, who lead regiments into battle. This Clone Trooper Commander minifigure appears in the AT-TE (set 75019), where he takes on a team of battle droids.

DATA FILE
YEAR: 2013
FIRST SET: 75019 AT-TE
NO. OF SETS: 1
PIECES: 4
ACCESSORIES: Long blaster

Helmet has breathing filters

Four yellow circles on armor chest plate

Black body glove is worn beneath white armor

Plain white legs have no printing

Long blaster gun is exclusive to LEGO Star Wars sets

Clone Trooper Commander
MILITARY RANKS

The clone pilot flies Republic vehicles in seven LEGO sets. His 2013 variant is the first to appear in a classic LEGO *Star Wars* set, rather than a Clone Wars set. This minifigure's unique armor includes specialist equipment for piloting tough missions, including a life-support pack and enhanced communications gear.

STAR VARIANTS
Hidden head
A Clone Wars variant of the pilot was released in four LEGO sets from 2008, with a similar but simpler design to later variants. A 2011 variant features a black head piece, rather than the tan piece just visible here.

Bigger belt
The 2013 redesign of the clone pilot is similar to the classic clone pilot, but he has a printed head and a more detailed helmet. The printing on his utility belt has also received an upgrade.

Clone Pilot
AIRBORNE WARRIOR

Helmet is printed with red Republic symbols and yellow markings that signify pilot status

Clone pilot wears life-support pack over standard Phase I clone trooper armor

Blaster offers protection if landing on a battlefield

Pilot in blue
A clone pilot in Phase II armor also takes to the skies in LEGO *Star Wars*. This minifigure first appeared in 2005 wearing a blue jumpsuit and white helmet.

2015 variant is the first clone pilot to feature leg printing

DATA FILE
YEAR: 2015
FIRST SET: 75076 Republic Gunship
NO. OF SETS: 1
PIECES: 4
ACCESSORIES: Blaster

Black rangefinder appears in only five sets—a bluish-gray version also appears on a similar variant released in 2008

The Clone Wars clone trooper has fought for the Republic in more than a dozen Clone Wars sets since 2008. His Phase I armor has been updated with a more stylized design and, unlike the earliest clone trooper minifigures, he has always had a face beneath his helmet instead of a plain black head piece. This variant appears only in the 2010 Clone Turbo Tank (set 8098).

Face of a clone
This flesh-colored head piece was first released in 2008. It is used for nearly all Clone Wars clone troopers.

A variant of this clone trooper, released in 2008, has identical torso printing, but its helmet does not have a rangefinder

STAR VARIANT
Signs of rank
High-ranking clone troopers often wear extra LEGO pieces over their basic white armor. Modifications include a visor shield that clips to the helmet, a shoulder pauldron to denote rank, and a kama blaster-shield around the waist.

White plastoid armor is blaster-resistant and lightweight

Utility belt holds survival gear, ammunition, and assault equipment

Clone Trooper
CLONE WARS SOLDIER

DATA FILE
YEAR: 2010
FIRST SET: 8098 Clone Turbo Tank
NO. OF SETS: 1
PIECES: 5
ACCESSORIES: Rangefinder, blaster rifle

Clone Troopers
PHASE I SPECIALISTS

These clone troopers carry out specialist missions for the Republic in several Clone Wars sets. They all wear Phase I LEGO armor and have identical flesh-colored clone trooper head pieces beneath their helmets. Some of these specialist troopers have unique armor markings, and all possess equipment that is crucial for their specific tasks and specialty missions.

Helmet fin helps to make jetpack trooper aerodynamic

This Clone Wars clone trooper helmet appears in ten other LEGO *Star Wars* sets

Clone Wars
Minifigures released in LEGO Clone Wars sets have been designed with a "cartoon" feel. These Clone Wars troopers have stylized torso patterns and brighter, bolder coloring than the classic LEGO *Star Wars* troopers (pp.4-5).

Utility belt with extra ammunition

Standard medium black blaster

LEGO jetpack piece is also used for the Mandalorian and Boba Fett minifigures

DATA FILE

NAME: Clone Jetpack Trooper
SPECIALTY: Aerial assaults
YEAR: 2009
FIRST SET: 7748 Corporate Alliance Tank Droid
NO. OF SETS: 1
PIECES: 5
ACCESSORIES: Jetpack, blaster

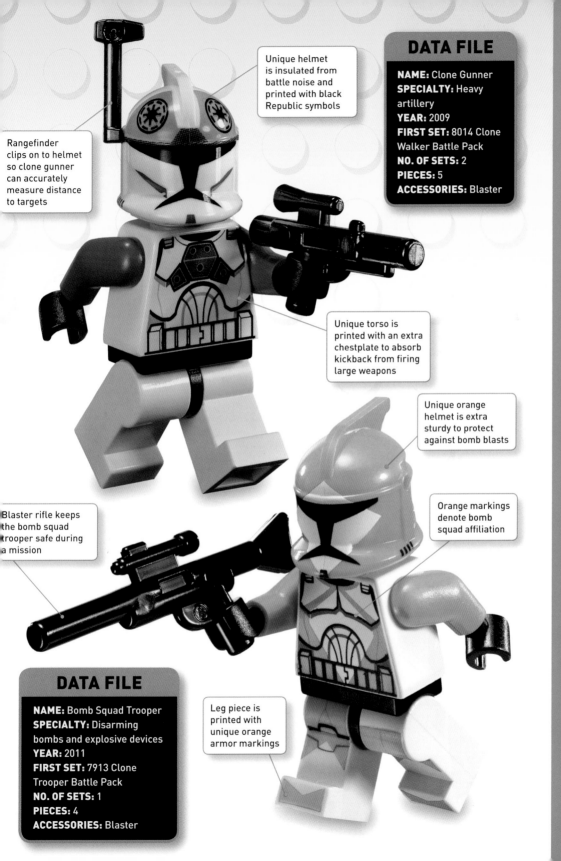

Unique helmet is insulated from battle noise and printed with black Republic symbols

Rangefinder clips on to helmet so clone gunner can accurately measure distance to targets

Unique torso is printed with an extra chestplate to absorb kickback from firing large weapons

Unique orange helmet is extra sturdy to protect against bomb blasts

Orange markings denote bomb squad affiliation

Blaster rifle keeps the bomb squad trooper safe during a mission

Leg piece is printed with unique orange armor markings

Clone Troopers
PHASE I SPECIALISTS

Leader of the Horn company, this clone commander is among Jedi Eeth Koth's guards onboard the Venator-class Star Destroyer, the *Steadfast*. His high rank is immediately obvious, thanks to the distinctive color and insignia on his armor. Such markings help distinguish between ranks in the vast army.

Clone trooper lieutenant
Given away with special promotions in 2013, this clone trooper lieutenant has a standard clone head rather than a stylized Clone Wars version. No other clone has his azure color markings.

Clone trooper commander
Released with the Clone Turbo Tank (set 8098) in 2010, this minifigure wears a striking piece of shoulder armor calle a pauldron. He share his visor with six othe clone models.

Green squad
Members of the Horn squad are known for their distinctive sand green markings. While 20 other clone minifigures share the same face as the clone commander, his printed helmet, torso, and legs are unique to this minifigure.

Green insignia identifies unit as Horn company

Twin blasters

Utility belt holds survival packs and extra ammo

Clone Troopers
PHASE I RANKS

Standard clone legs with green printing

DATA FILE
YEAR: 2011
FIRST SET: 7913 Clone Trooper Battle Pack
NO. OF SETS: 1
PIECES: 4
ACCESSORIES: Blaster

STAR VARIANT

Rangefinder Rex

For the Battle of Geonosis (set 7869), released in 2011, Captain Rex attaches a useful dark bluish-gray rangefinder to his helmet. In the 2008 AT-TE Walker (set 7675) and a promotional set of the same year, Captain Rex wears dark bluish-gray pauldron armor and has no rangefinder.

Clone Captain Rex serves under General Anakin Skywalker. The three variants of his minifigure feature in four LEGO sets, most recently the 2013 BARC Speeder with Sidecar (set 75012). He is not a typical clone underneath his helmet, as he has a unique LEGO head piece. Rex is heavily armored and carries two blasters making him particularly bold in battle.

Beneath his helmet with its blue battle honors and gray tally marks, Rex's head is printed with stubble and has a scar under his lower lip

Exclusive blue and black cloth pauldron is unique to this minifigure

Printing includes three ammo cartridges and welding marks where he has customized his armor

Unique torso printing, which continues onto the back, has tally marks to indicate Rex's victories

This Rex variant has leg printing for the first time

Rex wears an anti-blast black cloth kama around his waist to protect his legs from close-range blasts

Captain Rex
CLONE TROOPER CAPTAIN

DATA FILE

YEAR: 2013
FIRST SET: 75012
BARC Speeder with Sidecar
NO. OF SETS: 1
PIECES: 6
ACCESSORIES: Twin blasters

11

This band of brothers all have highly specialized roles and their own task-specific weaponry and equipment. Whether scouting enemy territory or tackling elite missions on the home front, they put themselves in the line of fire every day against the menace of the Separatists and their droid forces.

Advanced Recon Force (ARF) trooper helmet with red company insignia

Clone Troopers
SPECIALISTS

DATA FILE

NAME: ARF Trooper
SPECIALTY: Scouting enemy positions
YEAR: 2011
FIRST SET: 7913 Clone Trooper Battle Pack
NO. OF SETS: 1
PIECES: 4
ACCESSORIES: Blaster

Helmet rangefinder makes sure this specialist never misses his target

DATA FILE

NAME: ARC Trooper
SPECIALTY: Advanced combat
YEAR: 2012
FIRST SET: 9488 Elite Clone Trooper & Commando Droid Battle Pack
NO. OF SETS: 1
PIECES: 11
ACCESSORIES: Blaster

Long blaster rifle

Pauldron in dark red cloth

STAR VARIANT
ARF trooper
From the same set as the ARC trooper (left), this elite clone minifigure is the only one with this torso piece, which has dark red arms.

Red legs with blue and white armor printing is unique to this ARC trooper

Phase II clone trooper helmet. The striking red color is used on all gear connected with the Coruscant high command

Markings show the trooper is part of the elite Coruscant guard

DATA FILE

NAME: Shock Trooper
SPECIALTY: Speed and skill
YEAR: 2014
FIRST SET: 75046 Coruscant Police Gunship
NO. OF SETS: 1
PIECES: 4
ACCESSORIES: Twin blaster

STAR VARIANT

Shock trooper
From the 2007 Clone Troopers Battle Pack (set 7655), this shock trooper has a more rounded helmet with a plain black head piece underneath. His arms and legs are plain white.

Legs with red markings are unique to this shock trooper

Helmet is the same mold used for ARF Troopers, but in black with a silver printed visor

DATA FILE

NAME: Shadow ARF Trooper
SPECIALTY: Stealth missions
YEAR: 2011
FIRST SET: 2856197 Shadow ARF Trooper
NO. OF SETS: 1
PIECES: 4
ACCESSORIES: Blaster

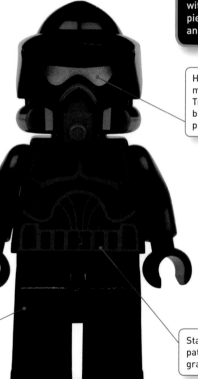

Mysterious minifigure
The Shadow ARF trooper of 2011 is truly intriguing. He only appears in the LEGO *Star Wars* galaxy!

The shadow ARF trooper was given away as part of the "May the Fourth be With You" promotion in 2011

Standard armor pattern is printed in gray on a black torso

13

Performing daring raids and rescue missions across the galaxy, these elite clone troopers will follow their Jedi commanders into any peril. Available in only a few LEGO *Star Wars* sets, they all wear Phase II LEGO armor, identifiable by the helmet shape and breathing filters. Their armor is customized—its color, symbols, and decoration reveal to which unit each wearer belongs.

Clone Troopers
UNBEATABLE UNITS

Long blaster

DATA FILE

NAME: 212th Clone Trooper
SPECIALTY: Frontline troops
YEAR: 2013
FIRST SET: 75013
Umbaran MHC
(Mobile Heavy Cannon)
NO. OF SETS: 1
PIECES: 4
ACCESSORIES: Long blaster

Unique legs with 212th battalion orange markings

Blue markings indicate this trooper is a member of the 501st legion

This minifigure appears in the AT-RT set (2013) and Z-95 Headhunter (2013)

Short blaster

Torrent force
The 501st is famous for including the renowned Torrent company, led by Captain Rex under the command of Jedi General Skywalker. It fights at the Battles of Christophsis and Teth, among many others.

Blue printing continues on legs

DATA FILE

NAME: 501st Clone Trooper
SPECIALTY: Frontline troops
YEAR: 2013
FIRST SET: 75002 AT-RT
NO. OF SETS: 2
PIECES: 1
ACCESSORIES: Blaster

Helmet with 501st legion blue pattern

Unique torso only appears on the pilot of the Z-95 Headhunter (set 75004)

Electrobinoculars

DATA FILE

NAME: 501st Clone Pilot
SPECIALTY: Areial combat
YEAR: 2013
FIRST SET: 75004
Z-95 Headhunter
NO. OF SETS: 1
PIECES: 4
ACCESSORIES:
Electrobinoculars

Headhunter
Wearing an exclusive helmet, this 501st clone pilot minifigure flies the 2013 Z-95 Headhunter (set 75004). His electrobinoculars can be stored in the plane's rear compartment weapon rack.

Wolf insignia on Phase II helmet

Dark bluish gray markings of Wolfpack unit

Short blaster

DATA FILE

NAME: Wolfpack
Clone Trooper
SPECIALTY: Rescue missions
YEAR: 2014
FIRST SET: 75045 Republic
AV-7 Anti-Vehicle Cannon
NO. OF SETS: 1
PIECES: 4
ACCESSORIES: Blaster

STAR VARIANT
Wolfpack clone trooper
The Phase I variant of the Wolfpack clone trooper has light blue arms and legs. He appears in the 2011 Republic Frigate (set 7964) and comes equipped with a jetpack that has twin nozzles.

Clone Commander Cody leads a battalion of clone troopers and reports to Jedi General Obi-Wan Kenobi. His minifigure wears clone trooper armor that has been modified to reflect Cody's unit and his rank as commander. He has appeared in two LEGO sets since 2008, in which he fights bravely during the Clone Wars.

Geonosian Starfighter (set 7959)
Commander Cody fights alongside Ki-Adi-Mundi in this 2011 LEGO set. They face a Geonosian starfighter, flown by a Geonosian pilot, which is fitted with a rotating cannon and opening cockpit.

Armor additions
Cody's minifigure comes with a gray pauldron that fits round his neck and a kama leg armor that clips under his torso. These extra pieces of armor designate Cody's rank as commander.

Commander Cody
OBI-WAN'S CLONE COMMANDER

Visor shield worn only by LEGO *Star Wars* clone commanders

DATA FILE
YEAR: 2011
FIRST SET: 7959
Geonosian Fighter
NO. OF SETS: 1
PIECES: 5
ACCESSORIES: Twin blasters

Unique helmet with orange commander markings

Orange markings denote Cody's affiliation with the 212th Attack Battalion

Cody wears the same basic armor as his fellow clone troopers, but his torso has orange arms and extra orange markings

Cody has been trained as an ARC trooper, so he is familiar with a variety of weapons

Separatist Spider Droid (set 7681)

The spider droid looks intimidating, but with such long legs, it isn't always stable, so Fox has a chance of winning this mighty battle.

Rangefinder feeds into a computer screen in Fox's visor

Commander Fox makes only one appearance in the LEGO *Star Wars* galaxy—in Separatist Spider Droid (set 7681) in 2008. He is well armed and armored for this battle against the huge, spindly Separatist spider droid. His minifigure has a unique red-patterned torso and helmet.

Distinctive helmet with dark red markings instantly identifies Fox

Blaster pistol

Extra protection

Commander Fox also comes with full shoulder protective armor. His torso has detailed printing on the back.

The red ranking stripes and decoration on Fox's unique torso and helmet represent his deployment on Coruscant

Dark bluish-gray anti-blast kama leg armor

Commander Fox
CLONE TROOPER COMMANDER

DATA FILE

YEAR: 2008
FIRST SET: 7861
Separatist Spider Droid
NO. OF SETS: 1
PIECES: 7
ACCESSORIES:
Twin blaster

Commander Wolffe is the tough leader of the elite Wolfpack clone trooper squad. His minifigure wears a helmet and armor printed with unique Wolfpack insignia and rank markings. Wolffe also has a unique face under his helmet, which sets him apart from the other clones in the LEGO *Star Wars* galaxy.

Clone Commander Wolffe
LEADER OF THE PACK

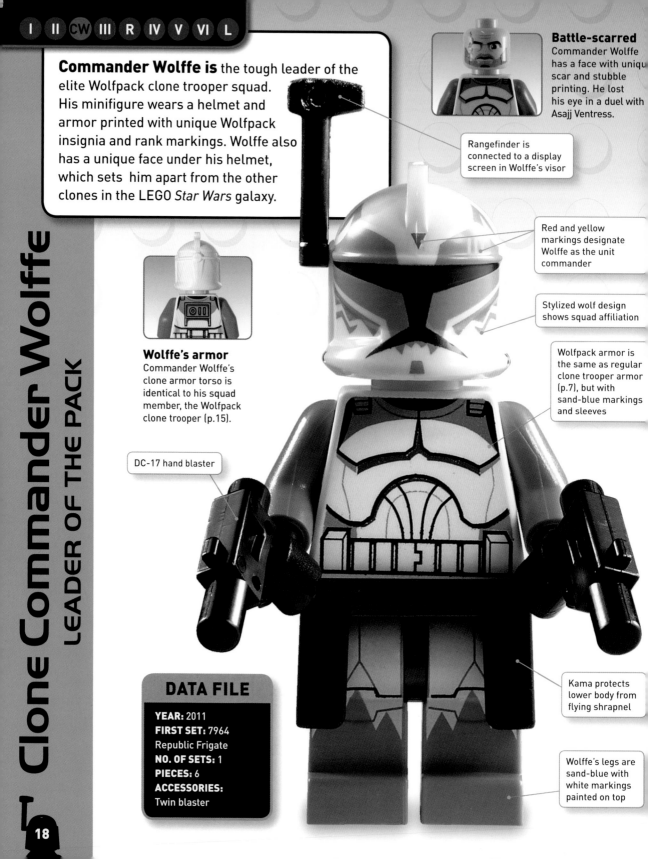

Battle-scarred
Commander Wolffe has a face with unique scar and stubble printing. He lost his eye in a duel with Asajj Ventress.

Rangefinder is connected to a display screen in Wolffe's visor

Red and yellow markings designate Wolffe as the unit commander

Stylized wolf design shows squad affiliation

Wolfpack armor is the same as regular clone trooper armor (p.7), but with sand-blue markings and sleeves

Wolffe's armor
Commander Wolffe's clone armor torso is identical to his squad member, the Wolfpack clone trooper (p.15).

DC-17 hand blaster

Kama protects lower body from flying shrapnel

Wolffe's legs are sand-blue with white markings painted on top

DATA FILE

YEAR: 2011
FIRST SET: 7964 Republic Frigate
NO. OF SETS: 1
PIECES: 6
ACCESSORIES: Twin blaster

Kashyyyk commander
This 2014 version of Commander Gree takes the AT-AP (set 75043) into battle at Kashyyyk, alongside an exclusive Wookiee minifigure, Chief Tarfful.

Leader of the 41st Elite Corps in the Clone Wars, Gree is one of only a handful of named clone commanders to become LEGO minifigures—the others are Fox, Cody, and Wolffe. Gree's dark green markings are unique but the same cannot be said for his face, which he shares with 20 other minifigures—all clones, of course.

DATA FILE

YEAR: 2012
FIRST SET: 9491
Geonosian Cannon
NO. OF SETS: 1
PIECES: 4
ACCESSORIES:
Blaster

Career
Though Gree is best known for his role in the Battle of Kashyyyk, as depicted in Episode III, his first appearance in minifigure form was as part of the Clone Wars Geonosian Cannon (set 9491).

Clone Wars Phase I armor made unique to this minifigure by its green markings, which denotes his rank within the 41st Elite Corps

The torso is a unique piece. Printing also continues on the back

Standard clone trooper leg armor has unique green printing

Commander Gree
ELITE CLONE LEADER

This loyal soldier of the Republic is wearing the enhanced Phase II armor that came in during the Clone Wars. Far stronger than the Phase I armor that preceded it, Phase II armor was the basis for the super-protective stormtrooper suits. This 2010 clone trooper from the 2010 Republic Swamp Speeder (set 8091) has no face under his unique helmet, just a plain black minifigure head.

STAR VARIANT
Trooper trouble
One of the seven minifigures that appears in the 2005 Clone Turbo Tank (set 7261), this is the first Phase II clone trooper. It has a plain black head beneath a helmet pattern that it shares with the aerial trooper in the same set.

Clone Trooper
This variant helmet is found only in the 2014 Clone Turbo Tank (set 75028) and the 2013 advent calendar.

Open T-visor in this clone trooper's helmet reveals a blank black head

Blaster rifle

Variants of this torso print are shared with other clone troopers, including one who wears a santa hat in the 2014 LEGO *Star Wars* Advent Calendar

Clone Trooper
PHASE II TROOPER

DATA FILE
YEAR: 2010
FIRST SET: 8091 Republic Swamp Speeder
NO. OF SETS: 1
PIECES: 4
ACCESSORIES: Blaster

Commander Neyo's minifigure proudly displays the emblem of the Advanced Recon battalion on his unique helmet and armor. Stationed on the arid planet of Saleucami during the Battle of Saleucami (set 75037), Neyo proves himself a loyal and efficient trooper— never more so than when he is ordered to execute Order 66.

Battle on Saleucami (set 75037)

Appearing in just one LEGO set, Neyo demonstrates his ability to pilot a superfast BARC speeder—a skill for which he is quickly gaining a stellar reputation.

Emblem of 91st Reconnaissance Corps

Some BARC troopers wear this sash

Reconnaissance gear kept inside well-stocked utility belt

Printing continues on the back and legs

Unique printed details on helmet help to identify this minifigure as Commander Neyo

It is rare to find minifigures with arm pieces of two different colors

Torso is unique to this minifigure

Commander Neyo
SALEUCAMI RECON COMMANDER

DATA FILE

YEAR: 2014
FIRST SET: 75037 Battle on Saleucami
NO. OF SETS: 1
PIECES: 4
ACCESSORIES: Blaster

These minifigures carry out specialist missions for the Republic in several LEGO sets. Many of these troopers have unique markings, such as the orange flashes on the armor of the 212th Battalion and the special camouflage pattern of Kashyyyk troopers. They may also carry equipment that is crucial for their specific missions.

Clone Troopers
SPECIALIST UNITS

Orange markings of 212th Battalion trooper

Scratches on armor

Only a few clone trooper minifigures have printing on legs

DATA FILE

NAME: 212th Batallion trooper
SPECIALTY: Ground attacks
YEAR: 2014
FIRST SET: 75036 Utupau Troopers
NO. OF SETS: 4
PIECES: 4
ACCESSORIES: Blaster

Helmet exclusive to Star Corps trooper

Pauldron in battalion colors

Undersuit visible below helmet

DATA FILE

NAME: Star Corps trooper
SPECIALTY: Ground attacks
YEAR: 2005
FIRST SET: 7261 Clone Turbo Tank
NO. OF SETS: 1
PIECES: 4
ACCESSORIES: Blaster

Battle gear
The Star Corps trooper is included in two sets between 2005 and 2007. In the 2007 Clone Troopers Battle Pack (set 7655), he appears without his pauldron.

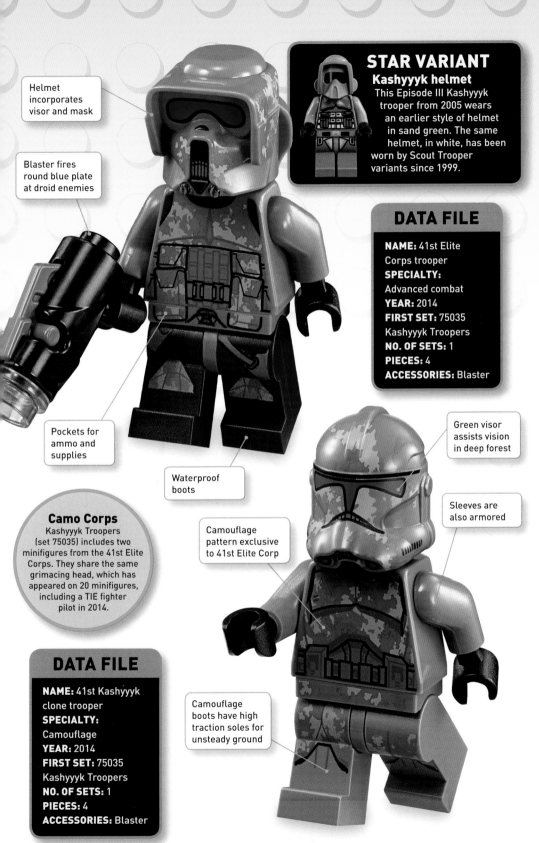

Helmet incorporates visor and mask

Blaster fires round blue plate at droid enemies

DATA FILE

NAME: 41st Elite Corps trooper
SPECIALTY: Advanced combat
YEAR: 2014
FIRST SET: 75035 Kashyyyk Troopers
NO. OF SETS: 1
PIECES: 4
ACCESSORIES: Blaster

Pockets for ammo and supplies

Waterproof boots

Camo Corps
Kashyyyk Troopers (set 75035) includes two minifigures from the 41st Elite Corps. They share the same grimacing head, which has appeared on 20 minifigures, including a TIE fighter pilot in 2014.

Green visor assists vision in deep forest

Sleeves are also armored

Camouflage pattern exclusive to 41st Elite Corp

Camouflage boots have high traction soles for unsteady ground

DATA FILE

NAME: 41st Kashyyyk clone trooper
SPECIALTY: Camouflage
YEAR: 2014
FIRST SET: 75035 Kashyyyk Troopers
NO. OF SETS: 1
PIECES: 4
ACCESSORIES: Blaster

These clone trooper minifigures are highly trained combat specialists. They are the elite forces that carry out vital and dangerous missions for the Grand Army of the Republic, and are seen in only a select few LEGO sets. Each clone trooper specialist wears Phase II LEGO armor with distinguishing colors or equipment.

Clone Troopers
CLONE SPECIALISTS

Orange stripes show the trooper comes from the 212th Battalion.

Scuff marks on helmet

Unique torso printing with ammo strap continues on the back

A clone armor skirt wraps around the paratrooper's hips

DATA FILE

NAME: Airborne clone trooper
SPECIALTY: Aerial assualts
YEAR: 2014
FIRST SET: 75036 Utupau Troopers
NO. OF SETS: 1
PIECES: 4
ACCESSORIES: Blaster

Audio pick-up for specialist communications

Green markings distinguish this minifigure as part of the 42nd Siege Battalion

DATA FILE

NAME: Siege Battalion trooper
SPECIALTY: Ambushing enemy fortifications
YEAR: 2005
FIRST SET: 7260 Wookiee Catamaran
NO. OF SETS: 1
PIECES: 4
ACCESSORIES: Blaster

Dark visor
Like ordinary clone troopers (p. 22), each of these specialized clone troopers has a plain black head, which can be seen through the open visor of his helmet so that the visor appears black.

Black body glove under white armor

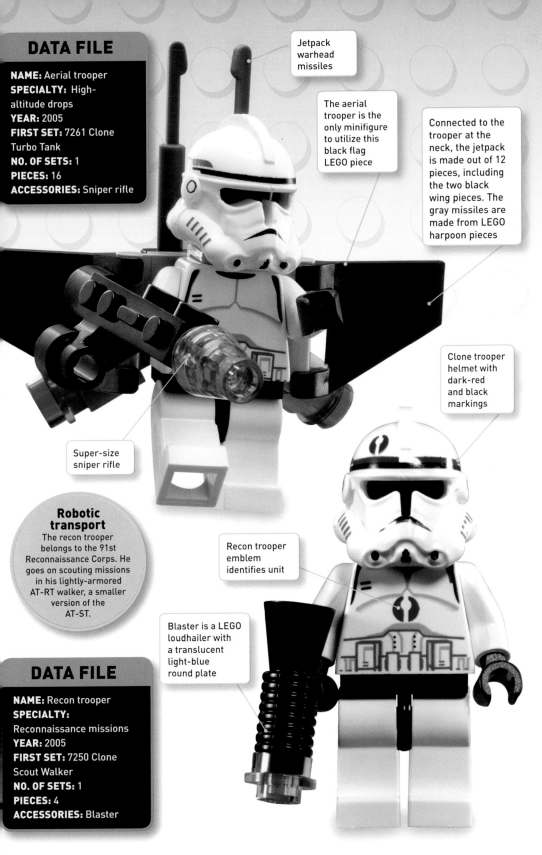

DATA FILE

NAME: Aerial trooper
SPECIALTY: High-altitude drops
YEAR: 2005
FIRST SET: 7261 Clone Turbo Tank
NO. OF SETS: 1
PIECES: 16
ACCESSORIES: Sniper rifle

Jetpack warhead missiles

The aerial trooper is the only minifigure to utilize this black flag LEGO piece

Connected to the trooper at the neck, the jetpack is made out of 12 pieces, including the two black wing pieces. The gray missiles are made from LEGO harpoon pieces

Clone trooper helmet with dark-red and black markings

Super-size sniper rifle

Robotic transport

The recon trooper belongs to the 91st Reconnaissance Corps. He goes on scouting missions in his lightly-armored AT-RT walker, a smaller version of the AT-ST.

Recon trooper emblem identifies unit

Blaster is a LEGO loudhailer with a translucent light-blue round plate

DATA FILE

NAME: Recon trooper
SPECIALTY: Reconnaissance missions
YEAR: 2005
FIRST SET: 7250 Clone Scout Walker
NO. OF SETS: 1
PIECES: 4
ACCESSORIES: Blaster

Clone Troopers
CLONE SPECIALISTS

The clone pilot is trained to fly the super-fast Republic and Jedi starships. His minifigure's uniform includes a jumpsuit, an armored torso with specialist equipment, and a high-tech helmet with communications system. This gray-suited clone pilot is unique to the V-Wing Starfighter (set 75039).

STAR VARIANTS

Face hidden
The clone pilot of the 2010 ARC-170 Starfighter (set 7259) wears the same plain helmet as the earlier pilot in V-Wing Fighter (set 6205) from 2006.

Shuttle pilot
This clone pilot flies Emperor Palpatine's Shuttle (set 8096). His torso and legs are the same as Captain Jag's minifigure (p. 27).

Helmet is marked with red and yellow Republic symbols

This is the only clone pilot wearing a gray flight jumpsuit

Helmet contains an air filtration system

Life-support pack integrated into uniform. Back of torso is also printed

White airtight flight gloves

Clone Pilot
FEARLESS FLIER

DATA FILE
YEAR: 2014
FIRST SET: 75039 V-Wing Starfighter
NO. OF SETS: 1
PIECES: 4
ACCESSORIES: Blaster

Clone Captain Jag is a soldier and pilot during the Clone Wars. His minifigure appears in only one set, ARC-170 Starfighter (set 8088) from 2010. He wears a blue jumpsuit and a life-support pack, common to pilot minifigures. His helmet has a unique design that only appears in this LEGO *Star Wars* set.

Clone pilots

Most generic clone pilots have a closed helmet or a white face mask (p.26). Two exceptions are the pilot who sits alongside Captain Jag (left) in the ARC-170 Starfighter (set 8088) and the 2015 Clone pilot (right) who flies the ARC-170 Starfighter (set 75072).

The blue pattern design on Jag's open-fronted helmet piece is exclusive to his minifigure

Helmet contains a life-support system because most starfighters do not have one on board

Jag sometimes carries a blaster

Orange visor helps with visibility when flying in bright light

Air supply hose

Jag's sand-blue legs also appear on Princess Leia in her original Endor guise

DATA FILE

YEAR: 2010
FIRST SET: 8088 ARC-170 Starfighter
NO. OF SETS: 1
PIECES: 4
ACCESSORIES: None

Captain Jag
CLONE PILOT

DK | Penguin Random House

Editors Pamela Afram, Hannah Dolan, Clare Hibbert, Shari Last, Julia March, Victoria Taylor, Ellie Barton, Matt Jones, Clare Millar, and Rosie Peet
Senior Designers Jo Connor, and David McDonald
Senior Slipcase Designer Mark Penfound
Designers Elena Jarmoskaite, Pamela Shiels, Mark Richards, Anne Sharples, Jon Hall, and Stefan Georgiou
Pre-Production Producer Kavita Varma
Senior Producer Lloyd Robertson
Managing Editor Paula Regan
Design Manager Guy Harvey
Creative Manager Sarah Harland
Art Director Lisa Lanzarini
Publisher Julie Ferris
Publishing Director Simon Beecroft

Consultants Jon Hall and Ace Kim
Additional minifigures photographed by Gary Ombler

First American Edition, 2016
Publsihed in the United States by
DK Publishing 345 Hudson Street,
New York, New York 10014
DK, a Division of Penguin Random
House LLC

Contains content previously
published in LEGO® *Star Wars*™
*Character Encyclopedia, Updated
and Expanded* (2015)

Page design copyright © 2016
Dorling Kindersley Limited

001–298872–Jul/16

A catalog record for this book is
available from the Library of Congress.

ISBN 978-5-0010-1389-1

Printed in China

www.LEGO.com/starwars
www.dk.com

A WORLD OF IDEAS:
SEE ALL THERE IS TO KNOW

Dorling Kindersley would like to thank:
Randi Sørensen, Robert Stefan Ekblom, Paul Hansford,
Heike Bornhausen, and Jakob Liesenfeld at the LEGO Group;
J.W. Rinzler and Leland Chee at Lucasfilm; Julia March,
Beth Davies, and Toby Mann for editorial assistance; Mik Gates,
Akiko Kato, Jon Hall, and Jane Ewart for design assistance.

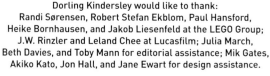